SCARBOROUGH IN THE 1930s &

by
Richard James Percy

1. Taking the waters 1930s style.

Front and back covers: Posters from advertising brochures issued by Scarborough Council during the inter-war years

For my mother and father

Published by Hendon Publishing Co. Ltd., Hendon Mill, Nelson, Lancashire.
Text © Richard James Percy, 1990.
Printed by Peter Fretwell & Sons Ltd., Goulbourne Street, Keighley, West Yorkshire BD21 1PZ.

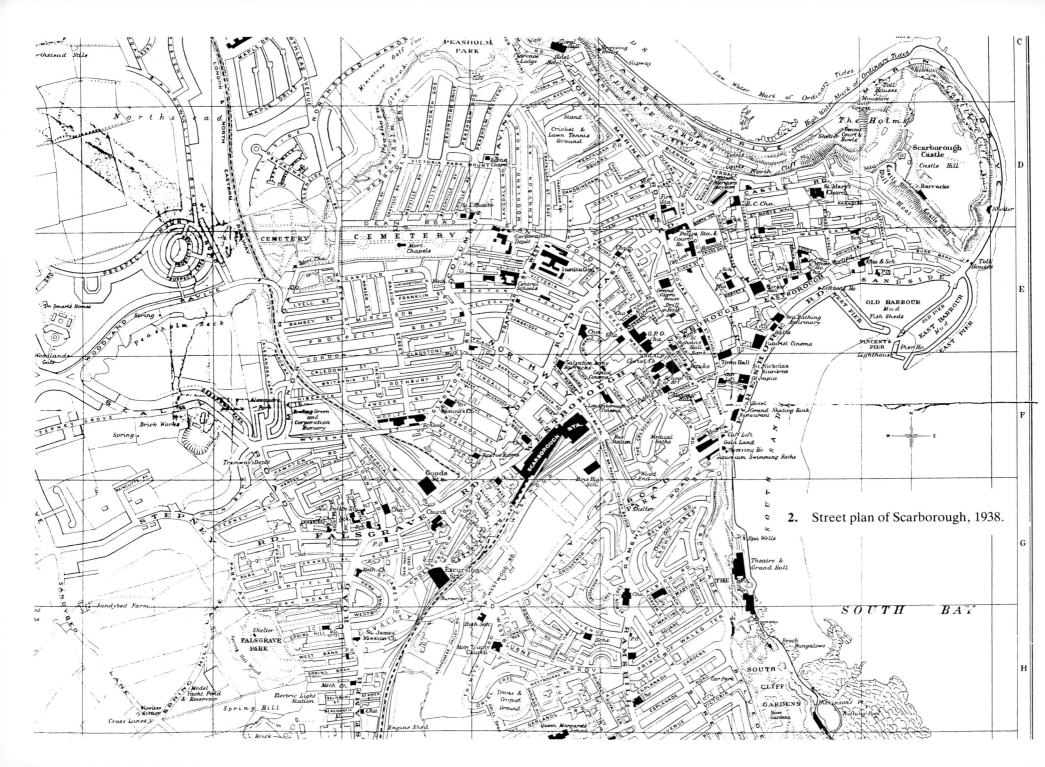

2. Street plan of Scarborough, 1938.

INTRODUCTION

Scarborough, described by Dr Granville the celebrated 19th-century Spa traveller as the 'Queen of the English Watering Places', lies in a unique position on the Yorkshire coast. There are magnificent views to the south, while to the north the Castle Hill with its ruined Norman battlements dominates the town. Its history is rich and varied. With the discovery of the Spa waters in the 17th century Scarborough became the haunt of Royalty and the landed gentry. It was the spread of the railways in the 1840s that put the town on the map as a holiday resort. The Spa waters declined in popularity and the well-to-do clientele were replaced by the middle and working classes who flocked to the coast to spend their well-earned wages.

The present century saw the town catering exclusively for the holiday maker. The Foreshore, until then a hive of fishermen's cottages and mast yards, was quickly turned over to the tourist trade. Amusement arcades, ice-cream parlours and fancy goods shops shot up at an alarming rate.

The years leading up to the Second World War witnessed large-scale development, a good percentage of which was intended to update the town and turn it into a premier seaside resort. Large parks and gardens were laid out and in an effort to popularize the North Side the Miniature Railway and the Open Air Theatre, said to be the best in the British Isles, were functioning in 1931 and '32. These were followed in 1938 by the opening of the North Bay Swimming Pool.

Large areas of the old town were demolished and although re-construction did take place, for the most part the resulting open spaces were turned over to car parks. The town expanded outwards and large estates sprung up at Barrowcliff, Briercliff, Edgehill, Newby and Northstead. By the end of the Second World War no large undeveloped areas of land could be found within the Municipal boundaries. The old hospital on Friarsway could not cope with the demands put upon it by the increase in population. In 1930 £50,000 had been raised towards a new building and the Board of Management felt that the time was right to go ahead with the new hospital. The foundation stone was laid in 1934 and two years later His Royal Highness, The Duke of Kent performed the opening ceremony.

The commencement of hostilities with Germany in 1939 saw the first batch of evacuees arrive in the town. Within two months over 12,000 children, their teachers and adults had been billeted in hotels, schools and private houses. By 1940 three-quarters of them had returned home, often at their own expense.

Throughout the war years Scarborough's beaches, cliffs and gardens were barricaded off with yards of barbed wire and other dangerous obstacles. Sentries were on patrol and it was a foolish person indeed that wandered off the marked path. Two fatalities did occur through not heeding the warning signs. What few holiday makers did arrive found it very difficult to get board and lodging as most of the hotels, apartments and large houses had been requisitioned by the military.

The first air-raid alert had sounded early in 1940 and what raids did occur were more on the tip and run scale and caused minimum damage. It was on the 18 March 1941 that Scarborough was subjected to an ordeal that taxed the Borough's wartime services to the full. What became known locally as the 'March Blitz' began about 8 p.m. with enemy planes flying over the surrounding villages of Flixton, Folkton and the Carrs dropping incendiaries at random. They closed in upon the town at 9.15 p.m. and remained overhead for about four hours dropping high explosive bombs, parachute mines and thousands of incendiaries, many of which bounced and spluttered down the Castle Hill creating a dazzling display. Many acts of bravery were recorded on that night with both civilians and the wartime services taking equal honours as they battled to rescue the trapped people. Scarborough was to endure many more raids but never again on such a large scale. By the end of the war there had been 317 alerts covering 411 hours. There had been 21 raids resulting in the dropping of 100 high explosives, several parachute mines and thousands of incendiary bombs. Forty people had perished and hundreds had been injured. Over 3,000 buildings had been either destroyed or damaged. These included Queen Margaret's School, the School of Art, the printing firm of E.T.W. Dennis & Sons Ltd., and Tonk's Furniture Repository.

Postwar planning concentrated upon the re-housing of families whose homes had suffered as a result of the war. German and Italian prisoners of war were drafted in to help erect the prefabricated houses that the Government had considered quick, cheap and easy to mass produce. Areas such as Commercial Street, which had suffered bomb damage, were allocated a number of these buildings but the main site was Sandybed where an extensive estate arose.

Another priority was the build-up of the holiday trade. The beaches and other restricted areas were cleared of their wartime obstacles and slowly the day trippers and holiday makers began to descend upon the town. The Spa, which before the war was the centre of high-class entertainment, re-opened but found it very difficult to live up to its former standards. The Scarborough Corporation purchased it a few years later and carried on the tradition of staging dances, concerts and shows.

Although the resort had emerged from the war slightly battle scarred it still retained its dignity. By gathering all its resources Scarborough had, at the end of the 1940s, once again resumed its position as one of the top seaside resorts in the British Isles.

3.   In 1875 a bandstand was built over the Spa Pump Room. Visitors could still descend the stone steps and take the waters although this service was abolished in 1890 for a more hygienic method. The bandstand which had become known as the North Orchestra was demolished in 1931 and the entrance to the wells blocked off. A kiosk was erected on the site and remained there until 1980 when a roundabout was constructed. The Pump Room still lies beneath the roadway and there has been talk of re-opening it. As yet there has been no positive response.

4.   During the bombardment by German warships in 1914 the Lighthouse was badly damaged, so much so that it was deemed necessary to demolish the tower. It was not until 1930 that the Scarborough Townsmen's Association came to the rescue with funds which they had raised through various events. This money was used to construct a new tower, the total cost being £2,250. Wednesday, 23 September 1931 saw the Lighthouse gaily decorated with flags and bunting. Large crowds had gathered on the piers to watch the Mayor (Alderman J. Butler) officially declare it working and the Mayoress unveiled a bronze plaque on the Lighthouse tower to commemorate the occasion.

5. This photograph shows the Toll-houses at the entrance to the Cliff Bridge as they were in about 1930. It was in 1826 that a group of people had banded together and formed a company with the desire to provide an easier access to the Spa. The result was the Cliff Bridge which was opened on 19 July 1827. To mark the occasion, and much to the consternation of the ladies, a mail coach and horses galloped at full speed, with a sailor balancing precariously on top, over the bridge. During the 1880s the bridge was altered and the Toll-houses erected. In 1951 the Scarborough Corporation purchased the bridge, abolished the tolls and in 1952 demolished the Toll-houses.

6. The Spa has always been regarded as the centre of high-class entertainment. This photograph taken in 1930 shows just how popular it was. Crowds would flock down to the Grand Hall to listen to Alick Maclean and his Orchestra. After his death in 1936 he was replaced by Kneale Kelley, conductor of the B.B.C. Theatre Orchestra. The present Spa building was designed by Thomas Verity of London and was formally opened by the Lord Mayor of London on Bank Holiday Monday, 1880. In the 1970s discussions took place as to whether the Spa should be demolished or refurbished. To the delight of many refurbishment was decided upon and the newly-restored building was officially opened on 23 May 1981.

7. The residents of Dumple Street and the adjoining Batty Alley are seen here posing for the photographer in 1931. Amongst the many faces can be seen Daddy Wood, in peaked cap and Little Helen, in V-necked jumper. To celebrate the demolition of this street an open-air party was arranged by the local shopkeeper Lizzie Richardson. At this party which was held in 1932 the guest of honour was Johnny Jackson the future Mayor of Scarborough. After the street was rebuilt it took the name Friargate.

8. Running parallel to Dumple Street was Cross Street, another narrow thoroughfare so typical of that part of the town. It is said that the street was named after the Market Cross that stood in the vicinity. At one time there were six public houses in what was not a very long street. The Wheat Sheaf and the Elephant and Castle were pulled down in 1850 to make way for the Market Hall. It was at the Elephant and Castle that the landlord, John Lawson, who only had one arm was hailed as the best billiard player in the district. Cross Street was demolished in 1933 and new flats erected.

9. On 5 August 1933 the Scarborough Aviation Display was held at Ganton Aerodrome, a small village on the outskirts of the town. Private aircraft arrived from all over the country to take part in the competitions. The Mayor and Mayoress of Scarborough were there along with the Lord Mayors of Hull, Middlesbrough and Wakefield. Scarborough's Rose Queen put in an appearance and Kathleen, Countess of Drogheda arrived at 2.30 p.m. to open the display. One novelty that drew the crowds attention was the Cierva Autogiro, the 'windmill machine' which soared and hovered at 2000 feet.

10. On July 1933 competitors in the Scarborough Trial and Rally organized by the Motor Cycle Club converged on the Marine Drive to be judged on their motoring skills. The tests were made up of reversing, braking and acceleration. After completing these manœuvres they then had to restart their motors and cover 100 yards and stop as quickly as possible after crossing the finishing line. At the end of the events there was a parade of all the vehicles with the judge awarding points solely for beauty and appearance.

11. Before the tractor was brought into service after the Second World War the launching of the lifeboat was an exhausting exercise. It had to be man-handled into the sea by a team of launchers and helpers. The first petrol-driven lifeboat, *Herbert Joy I* arrived in Scarborough in 1924. It had been a gift from Alexander O. Joy in memory of his brother who had drowned in the South Bay. This boat was replaced in 1931 by *Herbert Joy II*. It is said that the Scarborough Lifeboat service is the oldest in the country. In 1801 a boat had been built for the sole purpose of rescuing ship-wrecked sailors.

12. Posing for the camera in 1933 are the crew of the Scarborough lifeboat. Clockwise from the coxswain Jack Owston (top right) are – Jack Sheader, Frankie Sheader, Charlie Leader, Holden Sheader and Wyrill Crawford.

13.   This photograph of the Promenade Lounge which lies under the Spa Ballroom was taken in the early 1930s but if one was to have seen it in 1979 there would have been no drastic change in appearance. The Ballroom and Promenade Lounge were built to a design by Frank Tugwell, a local architect, in 1924. In later years the balcony on the right was boarded in and converted to a bar. During the early 1980s the Spa Refurbishment Project came into being. Three million pounds were spent on this project and the end result was a complex with all modern conveniences suitable to cater for the many conferences that visit the town every year. The original facade was retained which proved most popular with local and visitor alike.

14. Until its demolition in the 1930s Quay Street was an artists' paradise. The many 17th-century houses gave the street a unique atmosphere that no other street in the town possessed. The house facing the camera was originally the Dog and Duck Inn which was incorporated into the new Lancaster Inn in 1877. Today it is very difficult to tell which is original and which is reproduction on this building.

15. William Street was an area of tightly-packed tenements where one could see the gypsy and craftsman living together in relative harmony. Although many a scuffle did break out between the hawkers, dealers and the Irish navvies who lodged in the street a closeness did exist between the families. One feature of the street was the Model Lodging House where the homeless could sleep for 4d a night. There was 'Old Alex' with his ice-cream and hot chestnuts and 'Old Codge' the slaughterhouse man who sold a 3d worth of pigs fry or homemade black pudding. In 1935 a compulsory purchase order came into force and the area was demolished. The site remained derelict until 1962 when a car park was created.

16 & 17. What more could capture the elegance of an era than these two photographs, one taken in the Italian Gardens, South Cliff and the other on the rocks near the bathing pool. The young ladies parading in the gardens are mannequins from Marshall & Snelgrove Ltd., showing off the season's new line in dresses.

18. One of the many attractions intended to popularize the North Side was the construction of the Miniature Railway. This railway connecting Northstead Manor Gardens with Scalby Mills was opened on 23 May 1931 by the Mayor who was the first person to buy a ticket from the booking office. So popular was this railway that by the end of the first season over 400,000 people had been carried between the two stations. The engine *Neptune* was a scaled-down model of an L.N.E.R. Great Pacific class locomotive. Another which was named *Trident* came into service some months later.

19. Along with the Miniature Railway the North Bay Pool was another attraction built to draw the holiday crowds onto the North Side. Not all were in agreement with the project as the town already had the South Bay Pool. Nevertheless, work went ahead and on 4 July 1938 the Mayor officially opened the new pool. A musical programme was provided by Munn & Felton's Band and people flocked to see what was described as a 'wonder pool'. By night the pool was flood-lit with 42 under-water flood-lamps and the surrounding area with concealed lighting. During the 1980s the pool was modernized and became what is known as a Waterscene.

20. In the 1820s it was decided to erect a building worthy of being used as a museum, meeting house and library. Suitable land was found under the now St Nicholas Cliff and was purchased for £40. The stone to be used was given by Sir John Johnstone of Hackness Hall near Scarborough. The new building took the shape of a Rotunda on the suggestions put forward by Dr William Smith, the noted geologist. The new Rotunda Museum was opened in 1829. In 1861 the two wings were added to accommodate the growing collection. From its first opening the museum remained under the control of the Scarborough Philosophical and Archaeological Society until 1937 when it was taken over by Scarborough Corporation. The Rotunda Museum is now regarded as having the finest surviving interior of any other Georgian museum in the country.

21. The first cab to be seen in the streets of Scarborough was in 1836. By the turn of the century there could be seen over 200 horse-drawn cabs and landaus plying their trade in the town. After the First World War cabs declined in numbers and by 1936 only 20 remained. Cabman Frank Pottage can be seen here parked on Sandside in 1935. Today one solitary horse-drawn cab can be spotted battling its way through the heavy traffic on the Foreshore allowing the visitor a glimpse of a more sedate mode of travel.

22. The Scarborough Townsmen's Association was responsible for many spectacular events during the inter-war years. On 22 June 1936 one highlight of the 'House Party' programme staged by the Association was the magnificent display by the Royal Corps of Signals at Burniston Road Barracks. Although the rain poured down and at times postponement was contemplated the show went ahead watched by several hundred spectators. One event proved very popular. To the music of the band of the Royal Corps of Signals a large figure of eight movement was carried out by horsemen and motor cyclists who passed the centre alternately.

23. This view of the North Side taken in 1934 shows the marvellous sweep of the Marine Drive as it winds its way under the imposing Castle Hill. It had taken ten years to construct this roadway which was officially opened by the Duke of Connaught on 5 August 1908. In an effort to draw the crowds away from the South Side places such as the Corner Cafe, Northstead Manor Gardens and Peasholm Park were constructed in the 1920s and '30s. Today the North Side is very commercialized and attracts many visitors.

24. King Richard III House on Sandside is said to be the oldest building in the town. It was built about 1350 and was in all probability the home of Peter Percy the first Mayor of Scarborough. King Richard III is supposed to have stayed here on one of his trips north. In the early 1920s it was bought by a local man who turned it into a museum. It remained as such until the 1970s when a catering company opened it up as a restaurant. In 1989 it was re-opened as a 'House of Mystery' with interesting collections of memorabilia.

25. The British Tunny Club in Scarborough was formed in 1932 by such noted anglers as Colonel Stapleton-Cotton and Colonel E. Peel. Their headquarters was at 1, East Sandgate in what had once been the Victoria Inn. In the years between 1930 and 1954 when the last tunny to be landed in Scarborough heralded the demise of the sport, 227 fish were caught ranging in weight from 337lbs to 852lbs. There has been talk of re-forming the Tunny Club but as yet the response has been negative.

26. This photograph shows Globe Street in 1933. As with most of the 'down town' streets it was demolished in about 1935. Globe Street was originally called Stockdale Street from the name of the owner of the Old Globe Inn which in the 18th century became one of the first hotels in the town. It is said that the stables were used by the first Royal Mail coach to arrive in Scarborough. A poulterer would journey up from London to the Old Globe to supply the proprietor with his produce. At every luncheon ten to twelve dishes were served, one of which was always rabbit. In the rear yard of the inn the Freemasons built their Lodge in 1797. At the time of this photograph the Globe had become a Model Lodging House (the building with the porch) and remained so until its demolition.

27. This picturesque snow scene of Church Stairs Street was taken in the early 1930s. Notice the bulging walls of the cottages. It was in this street that John Wesley the founder of Wesleyan Methodism preached at the newly erected church in 1772. In the Rotunda Museum is a pane of glass from this church. On it is scratched, 'Watch and Pray, Wesley V.D.M.'. It is widely believed that Wesley himself wrote this. Today the steps still lead down to St Mary's Street but on either side are vast areas of grass where once the cottages stood.

28.   Each year from 1924 to 1939 there occurred in Scarborough one of the highlights of the season — the Procession and Crowning of the Rose Queen. It was part of the Battle of Flowers which was organized by the Townsmen's Association at the Spa. This photograph taken on 24 June 1936 shows the crowning of Miss Marie Panther, Rose Queen of 1936. At her side is Miss Kathleen Nicholson, the former Rose Queen. Miss Panther who was dressed in lacquer-red velvet and silver lame was crowned by Lady Patricia Latham. The band of the Royal Corps of Signals, the Braemar Girls' Pipe Band and the pupils of Miss Violet Adcock formed part of the programme.

29.   Scarborough celebrated the Silver Jubilee of King George V in 1935 by staging a series of events, one of which was the planting of oak trees in the town's public gardens. On 6 May the first official act of the ceremonies took place in the Prince of Wales Gardens on the South Cliff. Watched by a crowd of over 200 people the Mayor and Mayoress accompanied by other members of the Council placed the oak tree in the ground. In the background can be seen the Prince of Wales Hotel. Once noted for its high-class service this hotel, after two years of extensive renovation, has been converted into over 50 luxury apartments.

30. The Pavilion Hotel which stood adjacent to the Railway Station was a popular central feature of the town. It had been designed by William Baldwin Stewart and built in 1870. Perhaps its main claim to fame was that the film star Charles Laughton lived there for a time. It came as a great shock to many when it was demolished in 1970. Shown here on the steps of the Pavilion Hotel in 1938 is the hall porter, Mr George Pottage.

31. This view taken in 1934 shows Dr Rooke's Warehouse which stood opposite the Railway Station. As the name implies it belonged to the Doctors Charles and W.F. Rooke who were patent medicine manufacturers. In this building some marvellous concoctions were made up. There was cod liver oil, the Pills Elixir, Golden Ointment and Oriental Pills, all considered a boon for the nervous and afflicted. This building was demolished in 1935. The Victoria Hotel in the background is of interest as it was here that Charles Laughton was born in 1899.

32. This group of children from the Stepney Road area are all pupils of Mrs Walker's Dancing School. They are seen here in 1936 dressed up to celebrate Empire Day on the site of Robinson's Terrace, Scalby Road.

33. On 21 June 1936 the British Legion held a service in the Spa Grand Hall during the North Riding County Rally. After the service the British Legion laid a wreath on the sea. This ceremony was performed by a soldier who was carried on the back of a boatman into a small boat which then proceeded out to sea.

34. Here we see another view of Quay Street taken during the inter-war years. When demolition was in progress it was found that many of the houses had mooring posts in their cellars proving that at one time the sea must have lapped at their doorsteps.

35. Whitehead Hill leading down to Sandside has all been rebuilt except for the house shown on the photograph with the steps leading up to it. There has been a notable effort to re-create the original feel of the street.

37. In the 1830s Scarborough was noted as the first port on the east coast to begin trawling. By 1878 there were 62 trawlers fishing out of the port. Between the wars the steam trawler was already in decline. The last steam trawler to be seen in the harbour was in 1960 when the 118 ton *William Wilson* arrived. Twelve months later she was sold to a firm in Peterhead who were to use her as a salvage vessel.

36. The Scarborough Cavalcade of 1935 inspired various businesses, schools and organizations to dress up for the occasion. A local printer chose the theme of Empire for their contribution and here we see Miss Nellie Percy dressed up as Miss New Zealand on the steps of the Spa.

38.   At 9 p.m. on 10 October 1940 a lone enemy raider swooped over the Castle Hill and dropped a mine on the densely-packed houses of Potter Lane. Blasting a crater 60 feet across and 30 feet deep it damaged over 500 houses; 71 of which had to be demolished. Had it not been that many of the residents had been at a dance at the Olympia and a whist drive at a nearby church the death rate would surely have been much higher than the four fatalities that did occur.

39.   Short's Gardens suffered severe damage from the Potter Lane mine. It was decided to demolish the street completely and the new houses that were built on the site form what is today known as Castle Gardens.

40. On 18 March 1941 Scarborough suffered its worst air raid of the war. Shortly before 9.30 p.m. a large bomb fell on a terrace of houses in Commercial Street blasting them into a heap of rubble. Street shelters did not appear until a later date and consequently people had to find shelter the best way they could. Usually it was under the staircase as this was regarded as being the safest place. On this particular night this form of shelter did not prevent seven fatalities and many being injured.

41. For her outstanding courage when her home at 63, Commercial Street was destroyed by a bomb on 18 March 1941 twelve year old Margaret Willis was awarded the Gilt Cross of the Girl Guides Association. The ceremony took place at All Saints Church schoolroom, Falsgrave on 18 May 1942 and was presented by the County Commissioner Viscountess Downe. Margaret had been trapped with her family in the cupboard under the staircase and she had remained calm and cheerful throughout their long ordeal. They were finally rescued at 6 a.m. the following day.

42. During the blitz of 18 March 1941 a shower of incendiaries fell on the printing works of E.T.W. Dennis & Sons Ltd., in Melrose Street. The staff had been working until 9 p.m. and had only just left the building when the first bombs began to fall. Soon the premises were a blazing inferno and the war-time services had their hands full dealing with the conflagration. It was four months before production could start again.

43. On a quiet Sunday evening on 14 September 1941 a tip and run raider swooped low over the town and dropped two bombs, one of which fell at the side of the Woodlands Ravine railway bridge. The second fell on the pavement outside numbers 1 and 3 Prospect Mount Road. The houses crumpled up like paper and a 40-foot flame shot out of a ruptured gas main. It was most fortunate that no one in the houses were seriously hurt but a lady riding by on her bicycle was killed outright.

44.   A scene so typical of the war years of a wife seeing her husband off in the forecourt of the Railway Station. Note the white bands painted on the trees and kerbs to assist pedestrians in the blackout. In the background stands the Odeon Cinema which had first opened on 28 March 1936. The guest of honour had been Charles Laughton and the proceeds had gone to the Hospital Fund. In 1988 the Odeon was given listed building status and although now closed there are discussions in progress as to whether it could be used as a home for the Theatre in the Round.

45.   The rationing of clothing and footwear came into force on 1 June 1941 and every adult was allowed 66 coupons to last the year. As one can see by this advert for a top coat 16 coupons had to be surrendered along with the price of 79/6d. It is not surprising that shoppers were urged to go carefully with their coupons.

46. During the Second World War the strength of Scarborough's Special Constabulary was maintained at 302 members. They were trained in anti-gas measures, first aid and knowing how to deal with high explosive bombs and incendiaries. Shown here is a march past of the Specials on the Cricket Field, North Marine Road on Sunday, 2 August, 1942. Taking the salute is Lieutenant-Colonel Sir Frank Brook.

47. To honour the Green Howards association with Scarborough the Town Council conferred on them the Freedom of the Borough at a ceremony held at the Queen Street Central Hall on 2 November 1945. This allowed them the 'right, title, privilege, honour and distinction' of marching through the Borough of Scarborough on all ceremonial occasions with their bayonets fixed, colours flying and bands playing. They can be seen here marching along the Foreshore shortly before this honour was bestowed upon them.

48. With the commencement of hostilities with Germany in 1939 the natural fear was that a sea-borne invasion would occur. Scarborough hurriedly erected barbed-wire fences along the beaches, cliffs and Marine Drive. In many places mines were laid and people were warned that to venture into these restricted areas was tempting certain death. This photograph taken near the Corner Cafe on the North Side shows the typical wire entanglements.

49.   In May and June of 1940 the call-up of the Local Defence Volunteers or the Home Guard as they became known was under way. Captain J.P.S. Kitching had been appointed Company Commander and he had opened up a temporary office at the Old Hospital, Friarsway to explain to the volunteers what their duties would be. Posing for the camera are eleven members of the 10th North Riding (Scarborough) Battalion, Home Guard. From L to R front row are: Captain G. Holmes, Major A. Smith, Major J. Ellis, Captain A. Thornton and Captain A. Thompson. Back row: Second Lieuteant H. Jackson, Captain B. Jackson, Lieutenant W. Molyneaux, Lieutenant F. Unwin, Lieutenant W. Dent and Lieutenant J. Allen.

50. On 7 July 1943 the Scarborough Amateur Operatic Society staged *The Pay of the Pied Piper* at the Open Air Theatre. The lack of lighting owing to the blackout restrictions was more than made up for by the colourful costumes. Over 3,000 people turned out to watch this light opera in which out of a cast of 250, 200 were local children.

51. To celebrate the end of the war in 1945 street parties became a popular event. Seen here are the children of Friargate looking very happy after their festivities.

52. On 8 June 1946 large crowds had gathered on the south Foreshore to watch the Victory Day Drum Head Service to commemorate the end of the war in the previous year. The service which was held on the sands opposite the Olympia was attended by the Mayor, members of the Council, the 3rd Battalion, Green Howards and other representatives of the Armed Forces. The massed choir was conducted by Mr A. Keeton and Mr E. Robinson accompanied them on the Hammond organ. A huge wreath was taken on board the Lifeboat which then proceeded out to sea escorted by two whalers from H.M.S. *Hesperus* which was anchored in the bay. To the sound of the 'Last Post' the wreath was slowly lowered into the sea.

54. Home on leave at last.

53. At the height of the Methodist movement in the 1830s it was decided to build a chapel in Queen Street. Work went ahead and the new chapel was opened on 8 September 1840. In 1915 a fire broke out which destroyed Boyes Remnant Warehouse, much of Market Street and the Queen Street Chapel. It was not until 1921 that the foundation stone was laid for the new church which opened two years later. The centenary of the Methodist Church in Queen Street was to have been celebrated in 1940 but owing to the war had to be postponed until 8 April 1945; a day which saw large crowds congregating at the chapel.

55. In 1945 the entertainment got into full swing in anticipation of the holiday crowds.

56.   Donkey rides are one of the main traditional seaside attractions. As far back as the 1850s donkeys could be seen on Scarborough's beaches. In the 1920s and '30s a few of the well-known 'Donkey Men' included, Les Rodgers, Thomas Hodgson and 'Donkey' Elliot.

57. Scalby Mills on the North Side of Scarborough was until recently a quiet backwater with scenic views. The original building, called Low Mill, was burnt down in 1821. The new Scalby Mills became well known as a tea garden and refreshment room. In 1949 Scarborough Corporation took over the premises and undertook extensive restorative work. During the 1960s a new Scalby Mills Hotel was built and the old mill was taken over by a private firm who manufacture pottery.

58. The cosy atmosphere of the smoke room at Scalby Mills is shown here before the take-over by Scarborough Corporation.

59.   A scene so typical of the seaside is shown on this photograph taken on the south sands in the late 1940s. In the background can be seen the Futurist Cinema. Erected in 1921 it was said to be the best-equipped theatre in the United Kingdom. The organ had cost £5,000. On the ground floor was an American ice-cream and soda fountain which was the first of its kind to be seen in any place of entertainment. In 1957 the cinema closed and the building was taken over as a theatre.

60. This view taken on the Fish Pier brings back memories of the Scottish herring fleets which visited the port. It was not unusual to see over 400 boats in the bay. Following the fleet down were the Scottish herring lasses who would gather on the pier to gut the fish as it was landed. Today no herring fleets visit Scarborough and the fishing industry on the whole has been greatly affected by the Common Market restrictions.

61. Every September crowds gather on the pier to watch the Vicar of Scarborough bless the fishing boats. The large fleets of boats shown on this photograph taken in the late 1940s is a rare sight indeed today. Of interest is the Police Box on the left of the picture. It is the only remaining box left in the town and although the police still use it, it has really only been preserved as a reminder of the past.

62. The Punch and Judy man was once a regular visitor to the beaches of the resort. They faded out completely in the 1960s and '70s but once again Scarborough's holiday makers can enjoy, perhaps with nostalgia, the Punch and Judy man with his usual entourage of children give his tireless performance. One of Scarborough's best loved Punch and Judy men was Sidney Owenson who gave his first show here just after the end of the First World War. His motto in life was, 'A Punch and Judy man never makes a fortune, but gives a lot of happiness'.

63. The Lifeboat tractor which was introduced in 1947 was a great boon to the service which until then had had to rely upon a team of men to launch the boat.

64. This photograph of children playing in the water is taken at Scalby Mills Beck in the late 1940s. If one crossed the stepping stones and climbed the cliffs the views along the coast to Hayburn Wyke were breath taking. The whole area was a place of untouched beauty and was enjoyed by both young and old. The beck gurgled its way down the narrow glen and bubbled over the rugged boulders. At one time it had been a noted trout stream but by the 1920s had lost its popularity. During the 1960s Scalby Mills lost its rural setting as the promenade was extended and amusement arcades took over. What had once been a place of tranquil beauty now reverberated to the sound of seaside entertainment.

65.   Here we see a typical example of the type of house that made up the old town. This particular building went under the name of 'Crazy Cottage' owing no doubt to its lop-sided appearance. This area was demolished in the early 1960s.

66.   Regent Street, off Castle Road, was noted for its Mission Room. St Paul's Mission was erected in 1879 and could seat 300 persons. At one time the ground floor was used as a coffee and refreshment house. It was regarded as being the most popular church in the area and when it was learnt that it was to be demolished along with the street in the late 1950s the neighbours rallied round to try and save it – unsuccessfully in this case.

67. To celebrate this young man's 21st birthday on 28 March 1948 George Wardell and his Orchestra, resident band at the Cambridge Hotel, presented him with a key. The Cambridge Hotel stood on Ramshill Road, South Cliff but had to be demolished in the early 1970s owing to structural decay. In its place were built luxury flats.

68. North Street leading from Castle Road to Newborough was at the time of this photograph a very quiet thoroughfare. Running off to the right is St Thomas's Walk where the Spinsters Almhouses were situated. They had been built in 1841 by Mrs Elizabeth Clark, wife of a local shipowner. In the early 1980s the whole area was demolished and a vast car park created.

69. Foxton's Farm, Scalby Road, was at one time regarded as being in the country. The Falsgrave area was separated from the town by a mile of open common until the 1870s. Today it is what can only be described as a continuation of the town.

70.   This view taken of Ramshill Road looking down towards the Valley and the Foreshore shows the contrast in architecture which the town can offer to the interested party. Here on the South Cliff, once the home of Victorian respectability, one can see large mansions and villas, many of which have now been converted to hotels and boarding houses. South Cliff was originally called New Scarborough and was connected to the town itself by the Valley Bridge for which one had to pay a toll to cross. Today the area boasts nightclubs and public houses and has become very commercialized.

71. The town centre has changed drastically over the past five years. In many areas pedestrianized precincts have been created and are artistically laid out with seats and flower tubs. This view looking up St Thomas Street from St Nicholas Street, shows this part of the town centre as it was in the late 1940s. The building on the left is of interest as it housed one of the first libraries in the town. It then became a much-frequented coffee house. Today very little remains of the original St Thomas Street.

72. East Sandgate rising from Sandside to Tuthill is another street that has suffered in the name of modernization. The only house of note remaining is the former Tunny Club Headquarters. To the left and just off the picture is St Thomas's Church which was built in 1838 to a design by Thomas Davidson. It is a very simple building and possesses no tower. The last service was held some years ago and the premises taken over and converted into a museum.

73. Springfield Place leading from St Sepulchre Street is typical of the area. These solidly-built houses were condemned simply because they lacked all the modern conveniences associated with the 1960s.

75. It was a common sight on the south sands in the late 1940s and early '50s to see large queues of holiday makers waiting to have their weight read. It usually occurred on the day of their arrival and the day they went home.

74. Looking down from the Castle Hill onto the harbour the first thing to catch the eye is the old sailing vessel moored alongside the pier. At the backend of 1949 the Borough Council purchased the boat which had appeared in the film *Treasure Island* as the *Hispaniola*. It had originally been launched at Glasson Dock, Lancaster in 1887 as the *Ryelands* and had been in service until 1948 carrying bulk grain coastwise. On 1 July 1950 the Mayor, the Chairman of the Harbour Committee and the King and Queen Neptune, acted by Cyril Wells and Kathleen West from the Fol-de-Rols, officially opened the vessel's new aquarium. In 1954 the boat was taken to Hull where it was used as a museum. The old ship was last seen in the film *Moby Dick* starring Gregory Peck.

76. The year 1945 was the dawn of a new era. The war had ended and a whole new generation had entered the world.